BPD WORKPLACE PRODUCTIVITY 2.0

A PRACTICAL GUIDE TO STAYING POSITIVE, STAYING IN A JOB, GETTING ALONG WITH OTHER WORKERS, BE PRODUCTIVE AS A BPD IN THE WORKPLACE AND BRING OUT THE BEST IN YOU

LINSY B.

© 2019 Linsy B.

All rights reserved.

This book or any portion thereof may not be reproduced or used in any manner whatsoever without the express written permission of the publisher except for the use of brief quotations in a book review.

You are welcome to join the Fan's Corner, here

Disclaimer

The advice and strategies found within may not be suitable for every situation. This work is sold with the understanding that neither the author nor the publisher is held responsible for the results accrued from the advice in this book.

Dedication

This work is dedicated to Oje and Sem, without whose help, this book would not have come to light.

Introduction

People with borderline personality disorder invariably have a historical reputation for being unstable in the way they behave, think and feel about themselves and others. This book explains how their condition invariably tends to make them unable to perform well in most of the life spheres, especially the work environment and explains how best to deal with such situations.

They are characterized by spontaneous actions that include no consideration of what its outcome would be. Hence, employers' express hesitations employing people identified to have BPD, not minding how good or competent the person can be at the job. This is because of the general belief that they do not last in meaningful relationships, jobs inclusive.

This work centers on how people with BPD can be productive and also become better employees in any workplace they are in or any business they have to run.

It would provide a practical guideline on how persons living with BPD can stay and get along with colleagues at work and even excel at the job.

Table of Content

Introduction 3

Chapter One 6

    Personality Disorder 6

Chapter Two 11

    Borderline Personality Disorder (BPD) 11

    Borderline Personality Disorder Causes 12

    Diagnosis of Borderline Personality Disorder ... 14

    Effective Treatment of Borderline Personality Disorder 15

    Psychotherapy 15

    Drug Therapy Treatment 18

Chapter Three 20

    Certain Skills Used in Coping with Borderline Personality Disorder 20

Chapter Four 25

    BPDs in the Work Environment 25

Chapter Five 29

    Ways of Helping a BPD Employee or Coworker 29

    How to Help an Employee with BPD 30

Role of Employer on BPD Employee 31

How Coworkers can Help BPD Employees 35

Chapter Six 38

Certain Rights Enjoyed by an Employee with Borderline Personality Disorder 38

Chapter Seven 42

Steps on Being Productive as a BPD at the Workplace .. 42

Creative Ways of Handling Some BPD Symptoms 52

Conclusion 55

Chapter One

Personality Disorder

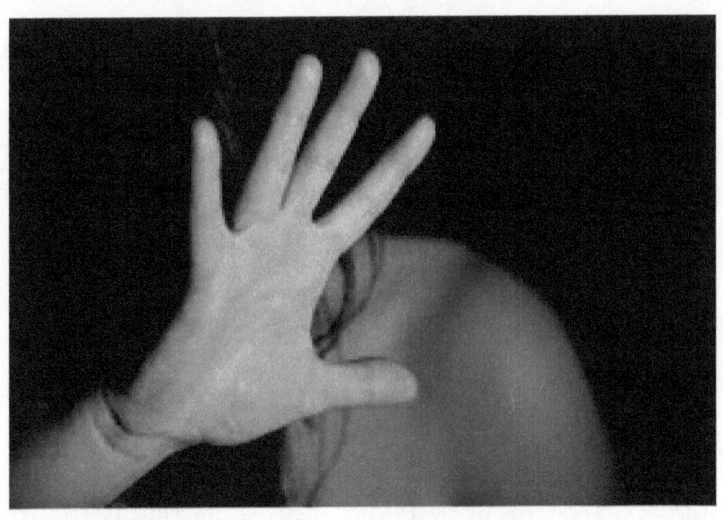

For one to properly understand what Personality Disorder is, it would be necessary to start grasping the meaning of 'Personality'. There are quite many ways to define personality, none of which is a universally accepted way of defining it.

Personality can be used to refer to a person's unique pattern of traits or the most effective way of accurately describing a person's behavior in all its detail. Some persons like describing a person's personality as the way a person's psychology can be used to explain the behavior consistency displayed by an individual when confronted with different situations. It is this behavioral pattern that leads people to associate an identity to a person which can be recognized by more than one objective observer as the way a person act. Simply put, it is an assumed role or behavioral pattern expected of an individual in certain situations and can undoubtedly be recognized.

This distinct personality is usually deeply ingrained in the person in ways that they have very little control over, so that their complex pattern of social behavior that typically includes the way they perceive, relate, self-esteem and live amicably in their environment is either enhanced or hampered by this personality trait. This behavior invariably tends to affect the overall behavior of a person to themselves, others around them and to the environment.

A personality disorder can best be described as a mental health condition that causes a person to acquire a fixed, abnormal or unhealthy pattern of acting, responding to issues, thinking or functioning. An individual with a personality disorder does not perceive or relate to things, people or situations as expected, they have trouble with doing this. A lot of people with this condition do not know that they have a problem, but rather blame others for their challenges since they perceive their own actions as being natural. This ends up causing significant problems and cognitive limitations for them in collaborative relationships, work, school, and other social spheres. These disorders typically start at teenage or early adulthood, though in some situations it may not be obvious.

Personality disorders are said to be egosyntonic and not a neurotic disorder. It can be caused by both environmental and biological elements. This means it can be genetic or can be triggered by life experiences. Unlike some mental conditions, personality disorders are never a direct result of accidents or apparent injuries to the brain. Disorders of this type can disrupt the way these people typically live their life and that of the people around them. One common thing with many personality disorders is they tend to all be characterized by a deviant and odd way of thinking or behaving. Common personality disorders include;

- Paranoid Personality Disorder (associated with having trust issues, tend to always suspect peoples' motive)

- Schizoid Personality Disorders (highly uninterested in personal or social relationships)
- Schizotypal Personality Disorder (have strange, frightening experiences that sometimes include the hearing of voices.)
- Borderline Personality Disorder (possess an extreme impulsive way of reacting to issues.)
- Histrionic Personality Disorder (attention-seeking)
- Antisocial Personality Disorder (disregard for people's feelings)
- Avoidant Personality Disorder (extremely sensitive to rejection, corrections or criticism)
- Narcissistic Personality Disorder (Egocentric individuals with a strong belief in being special and more important than others around them)
- Dependent Personality Disorder (Tend to be clingy and excessively dependent on others. They have an insane sense of entitlement.)
- Obsessive-compulsive Personality Disorder (extreme perfectionist and control freak)

Personality disorders are usually recognized in early adolescence years and the changes keep developing up to early adult life; then become less obvious in late adult years. The leading risk factors for personality disorders are family history, traumatic or chaotic childhood, or variations in brain structure and chemistry. Having known the different personality disorders, we would concentrate on borderline personality disorder which is the primary focus of this book.

Chapter Two

Borderline Personality Disorder (BPD)

Borderline personality disorder (BPD) is a mental sickness that is characterized by a consistent pattern of varying moods, actions, reactions, feelings, self-image or thoughts, that impair the way one thinks and feel about themselves and others, resulting to impulsive actions, problems in relating and dysfunction in their conventional life.

People with BPD are faced with a constant experience of instability in the way they see themselves, in their mood or how they feel or act. A BPD person is prone to unstable and intense feelings as they tend to always act spontaneously, based on how they feel at the moment of the action, not minding what the outcome would be. Some of these impulsive actions could be; having unprotected sex, binge eating, self-injury, gambling, suicidal thoughts or behaviors, quitting a job or a relationship.

A person living with BPD is characterized by unstable behaviors with a high fragile self-image, intense fear of being abandoned or lonely, severe swings in mood, a strong sense of emptiness. Some other issues associated with persons with BPD prominently include an intense display of anger and even stress-induced paranoia. A BPD person's aims and internal preferences are usually unclear and disturbed. They are repeatedly confronted with the dilemma of 'who am I?'

Borderline Personality Disorder Causes

The possible causes or development of BPD is relatively complex and there are a variety of possible causes, which can be genetic, biological, or environmental influences.

However, scientists have been unable to identify the exact causes of BPD. However, some attempts have been made to classifying the causes of BPD into;

Environmental Factors

By environmental factors that can cause BPD, we mean life experiences of the person, which could have triggered the disorder. Experiences like distressing childhood or maltreatment, early separation from parents or caregivers, physical and sexual abuse, emotional or physical neglect or even insensitivity of parents. There is a huge possibility for a child from an emotionally invalidating environment (an environment in which a child's emotional needs are unmet) to develop BPD. This does not mean every child who has a similar encounter would have BPD, or that someone who did not have these experiences cannot have BPD.

Genetic and Contributing Biological Factors

Studies have shown that Borderline Personality Disorder runs in some families than in others, even then it is not clear if this is a result of environmental or genetic factors. It has been noted that a variation in the gene which controls the brain's use of serotonin may be related to BPD. Serotonin is a natural chemical in the brain. The study shows that individuals that have this particular kind of serotonin gene may likely develop BPD if they experience distressing childhood events. BPD has also been associated with excessive activity in the parts of the brain, which is in charge of experience and expression of emotions. For instance, it has also been noted that people with BPD have a high activation of their limbic system (which controls the brain's perception of fear, anger, and aggression) than people without BPD. This results in their constant bout of emotional instability.

Diagnosis of Borderline Personality Disorder

Diagnosis of BPD is often done in adults than teenagers since some of the traits seen in teens tend to be categorized as youthful exuberance which many tend to believe will diminish as they start getting older. Some ways of diagnosing borderline personality disorder are;

- Discussion of signs and symptoms
- A detailed session with a doctor or mental health provider
- Medical history and cross-examination

- A psychological evaluation which may include the use of questionnaires.

Effective Treatment of Borderline Personality Disorder

Just like other personality disorders, BPD patients also have the hope of recovery from their ordeal. Though it takes time, with logical consistency in the treatment procedures, a BPD patient can be whole. Treating BPD helps the patients learn ways they can manage and cope with their condition; it also makes them feel better about themselves and try to live a stable life pattern. The major ways of treating BPD are Psychotherapy and Drug therapy.

Psychotherapy

Psychotherapy also known as 'talk-therapy,' is a treatment for people with mental or emotional conditions using dialogue. It is believed to be the most basic approach in the treatment of borderline personality disorders. This treatment primarily focuses on increasing the patient's ability to function and manage the emotions that cause them to feel uncomfortable. The therapy is typically aimed at helping the BPD improve their interpersonal relationships by recognizing their feelings and that of others better, enlightening them to reduce their impulsive reactions in the process.

This is achieved by causing them to observe their feelings rather than obey their gut feeling of immediately acting on it, and lastly is getting the BPD patient to know about their mental condition. Various forms of psychotherapy are known to be able to offer tremendous help in the treatment of borderline personality disorder. Some of them include;

Dialectical Behavior Therapy (DBT)

DBT is a group or individual therapy designed specifically to treat borderline personality disorder. It does this by helping patients better manage their emotions, stress and other BPD symptoms through the use of a skill-based method of advising patients on the best ways of improving the way they relate with other people.

Mentalization-Based Therapy (MBT)

This approach tends to employ a system talking as its way of therapy that helps the troubled persons identify their own thoughts and feelings as soon as these thoughts arise so that they are better equipped to develop an alternate perspective on the situation. MBT typically tends to emphasize on thinking before reacting.

Schema-focused Therapy

This type of therapy tends to focus on assisting people either at the individual or at the group level. It tries to help BPD patients by enlightening them on how best to identify some of their yet to be satisfied needs in their lives that have contributed to their negative life patterns. It also helps them track some of their bad behaviors, especially if such behaviors were useful at some point in their lives for their survival, but are presently no longer used, and are rather now becoming a source of harm in many areas of their life. The principal focus of this therapy is typically aimed at helping the affected person craft a way to realistically achieve their life ambition in a lot more healthy and creative ways.

Transference-Focused Psychotherapy (TFP)

This is also referred to as psychodynamic psychotherapy. The key aim of TFP is on helping individuals better recognize their emotional and interpersonal difficulties in the way they can relate to the therapist. The insights from this therapy can now be used by the person with BPD to handle various ongoing situations in their life.

Systems Training for Emotional Predictability and Problem-Solving (STEPPS)

STEPPS uses a 20-week treatment approach that generally involves the specific persons working in groups that also incorporates the family members friends, caregivers, or significant others of the patient, in the treatment plan. STEPPS is frequently combined with other types of psychotherapy for it to be more effective.

Good Psychiatric Management

The focus of this treatment revolves around trying to make sense of emotionally challenging moments by considering the interpersonal context for the feeling experienced. To achieve this, it tends to use a combination of case management, treatment anchors where the patient participates in their work or school activities. It may integrate medication groups, family enlightenment, and individual therapy.

Drug Therapy Treatment

There are presently no known drugs approved for the treatment of borderline personality disorder even though certain drugs can help with certain symptoms like aggression, depression or anxiety. Antidepressants are also often used on patients that have major episodes of depression as one of the symptoms they display as a result of their BPD. Patients can occasionally use antipsychotics, carbamazepine or valproate, lithium when they experience impulsivity or aggression. Note that drug therapy is not the most satisfactory form of treatment for BPD, and not to be considered a first choice. It is rather considered when the patient is experiencing a notable episode.

A BPD patient can also be hospitalized in a psychiatric hospital, as this can help keep them safe from suicidal gestures and self-injury.

Chapter Three

Certain Skills Used in Coping with Borderline Personality Disorder

For people who experience BPD symptoms, you will want to practice soothing techniques and self-help tools that can also assist in the recovery process. To go down the recovery path, they are many adapting techniques that individuals can use in the feelings that come with being hopeless and isolated.

Here are some forms of coping skills that have worked for many people;

General Comforting Techniques to Try

- Cuddling a teddy bear
- Singing or humming a song
- Having a bubble bath
- Having a drink that causes soothing effects
- Playing around with the lights
- Play and listen to some soothing music that put you to sleep
- Put on comfortable clothes
- Make your bed and change your bedsheets
- Write and read your diary
- Speak with an empathic person
- Call a sympathetic person
- Walking a dog or patting a pet
- Hug someone or yourselves
- Motivating yourselves
- Visit a secure place
- Eat a quality and nutritious meal
- Pick fresh flowers
- Self-comfort when distressed

- Say a quiet prayer
- Practice medication
- Indulge in mindfulness
- Learn yoga and effective breathing techniques
- Install and use mobile apps that have soothing effects

Interrelationships Tips for the Workplace

- Move away from potentially toxic situations than saying something you will regret
- Apologize for any situation that warrants an apology
- Discuss boundaries with a partner and make efforts to stick to it
- Show restrains when feeling rage by moving away until the feeling passes away
- Identify potential triggers and discuss with partners to address it

Maintaining a Positive Outlook

- Respect and keep regular appointments with support networks, even when feeling okay
- Following through with prescribed medication
- Reach out frequently to supportive friends or family members who are trustworthy
- Eat healthy food, even when uninterested

Activities that Help Calm the Brain

- Relax and stay calm
- Try and meet other people to stay distracted
- Comfort and taking care of yourselves
- Indulge in activities that calm and distract you
- Staying focused
- Expressing and responding to intense emotions in a controlled and calm way

Focusing Methods

- Perform a body scan to identify what you are feeling in your body
- Identify five things around you can hear, see, and feel
- Do feelings check to identify your immediate feelings

Crisis Management Techniques

- Take the medication prescribed for when necessary situations
- Kick objects that are not harmful around
- Cry yourselves out
- Create a personalized crisis plan even when there is no crisis
- Contact someone who understands how you feel

Activities that Distract

- Gardening
- Play board games and participate in other hobbies
- Watch a movie or any interesting program
- Walking, strolling, jogging, running, dancing, and other exercises
- Visiting the beach

Anger Management

- Find a private place to scream yourselves out
- Shake yourselves as a dog would
- Punch a pillow
- Indulge in very rigorous exercises

Chapter Four

BPDs in the Work Environment

People tend to view persons living with borderline personality disorder in the work environment different from how others are viewed. Generally, BPD persons are known to be bad at sustaining relationships, as they find it difficult to easily fit in, so, it is believed that people living with BPD do not relate well with workers or even superiors at work, they do not concentrate on work activities, often absent or tardy, needs extra time and attention to learn, lacks stamina to work and do not accept difficult tasks. Most of these beliefs are assumptions made by colleagues. Some of the major issues or problems of BPDs in the job place are;

Intense & Unstable Personal Relationship

A BPD's initial feeling towards a job, co-workers and employer are often intense and idealized. He or she sees them as doing no wrong (perfect), and also as close friends or buddies who love them a lot. However, when the scale falls off, these feelings end and gives way to negative thoughts. The BPD person ends up not seeing anything good about the colleagues rather see them as enemies, out to get him or her. They see co-workers as not being supportive, backstabbers and haters who do not care about them. This devaluation occurs as a result of an overpowering sense of rejection or abandonment. This feeling can happen slowly or even faster than expected. This particular issue poses a big threat at work for the BPD person, as the co-workers are no longer free with someone who sees them as an enemy. This could cause the BPD person to be laid off or even voluntarily resign from the job, because they now begin to see the environment as a place filled with enemies.

Splitting

Splitting is a mechanism for defense that people living with BPD develop as a way of managing their erratic emotions. Their emotional reactivity makes them see people as either 'all good' or 'all bad.' Instead of BPD persons to see people as primarily good with few bad traits, they see people as entirely bad; this feeling is developed all in a bid to avoid any possibility of rejection or abandonment. Once a BPD's perception changes from appreciation to devaluation, they are totally consumed by anger and forget that they ever felt differently towards these same people. With this, they may end up playing co-workers against each other, spread gossips, or even unload their stress and drama on their colleagues, without realizing the effect their actions may have on the working environment.

Sensitivity to Rejection

A BPD will always tend to display an excessive sensitivity to any form of rejection he experiences. This usually tends to trigger in them the thoughts of not being loved at work, thereby affecting their productivity at work. Their hypersensitivity towards the environment causes them to feel that others are bent on humiliating them, so working on a team project induces a competitive attitude, instead of team spirit of cooperation because of the desire to be recognized and not rejected. A little correction or admonishment by a boss or co-worker could be interpreted as humiliating or a target to get him or she fired. They see other people's actions as a means of rejection, making their attitude towards work, and coworkers go down until they are let go as usual.

Impromptu Resignation

Another possible trait of BPDs is a history of sudden resignation and change of jobs. This is due to an unstable sense of identity or goals.

Chapter Five

Ways of Helping a BPD Employee or Coworker

No matter how hard a person living with borderline Personality disorder tries to do things right, if the people around the person do not try to assist the person, the whole exercise could become futile. It is important therefore that we also consider how the colleagues and fellow workers can also play their role in helping them achieve this great task of being the best possible person they can be, and then we can dive into the practical guidelines that can help a person living with BPD become the best they can be at the workplace so that they can become more productive.

How to Help an Employee with BPD

The personality of a BPD person tends to create negative vibes in the workplace, especially if the persons around them do not know how to manage them properly. Their impulsive nature, intense emotions and erratic nature can be a turnoff, and lead to disaffection amongst coworkers. However, a healthy working environment can provide stability in the lives of people living with this disorder. Employers and coworkers are often not knowledgeable enough to know how best to deal with workers diagnosed with BPD, and this makes them often unprepared to handle the traits displayed by an individual with BPD. Not many people realize that a workplace can actually provide a BPD individual with the much-needed stability and goal orientation they would need. The first step employers and coworkers should take to help a worker with BPD is to study and understand the mental condition and its underlying psychological features.

We would be taking this section into two parts; how an employer can help the BPD employee and how coworkers can help a BPD colleague.

Role of Employer on BPD Employee

As an employer, it is important to an employee with BPD that the working environment is as stable as possible. To start with, it is essential that limits are set, and the work ethics expected of them are properly defined and understood. This would help in curbing the BPD employees' impulsive reactions and enable them to know what is expected of them at the workplace. This code of conduct should be seen by all parties to be fair, so that no one, especially those with BPD does not begin to feel that they are being targeted and that the rules are specifically made for their sake.

It is also important that a system is put in place for conflict resolution, interactions and the reporting of complaints by any party who feels aggrieved about a situation that should also be strictly adhered to.

Another often overlooked aspect of ensuring that the work environment does not become toxic is in how meetings are handled. It is important to ensure that they are not allowed to deteriorate into arguments that can sometimes end up making a person with BPD feel there is a gang up against him or her.

Employers should also be aware that individuals with BPD tend to have periods of unrestrained outbursts of protest even when there is no justified cause for it. This information is very important so that the employer, senior colleague or supervisor can be better prepared to deal with such situations, by not trying to outdo them in the outburst match or display of anger. In such situations, it will always be better to try to use calming and encouraging words.

Always try to validate the emotions of the employee rather than their perception. Use expressions like "I understand you", "I get how you feel", "I hear you." But remain civil and ensure boundaries are not crossed. Do not forget that many BPD persons tend to have the ability to be manipulative with their emotions, which is why the setting of boundaries beforehand and applying them is very important. The followings are possible steps an employer can take to help make the working place suitable for an employee with BPD;

- Develop clear, written work procedures that can be enforced fairly on all workers
- Encourage employees with BPD to always attend their counseling or psychotherapeutic appointments. Where possible, you can adjust their work schedule to make it possible for them to meet up with their appointments
- Allow employees with BPD to make calls to their therapists and others capable of providing them the needed support
- Encourage the use of breaks and holiday hours
- Break assigned job tasks into smaller unit of jobs
- Make daily "TO-DO" lists and check items off as they are completed
- Provide written checklists and instructions
- Allow the employee certain breaks where the employee with BPD can be allowed to work from home on certain days
- Allow employees to play soft, quiet relaxing music at their workspaces
- Offer appropriate praise and reinforcement for positive work interactions

- Ensure they are kept active during work hours to reduce the urge to relapse into some of their associated symptoms
- Have a system in place to serve as a form of Program for Assisting Employees and encourage them to use it
- Encourage all employees to stay focused on their job in the work environment
- Have regular one on one meetings with employees and use the opportunity to discuss workplace-related issues and performances.
- Use project calendars to mark meetings and deadlines
- Have clearly defined and written long and short-term goals
- Organize sensitivity training for all employees and supervisors on how to work harmoniously with fellow workers

With these steps, an employee with BPD will feel a lot safer and be able to stay longer and also be productive in the workplace. Now let's move to the second part of helping the employee with BPD.

How Coworkers can Help BPD Employees

Coworkers of individuals with BPD should be made to understand how challenging it can sometimes be to interact with them. The disruptive behavior they exhibit sometimes happens frequently, which tends to make it very difficult to live in peace with their drama. It is therefore important that coworkers understand that they are expected to show more empathy and a little more understanding in dealing with their BPD colleagues.

Criticism is one major action that a BPD person is unequipped in handling because of the tendency to trigger a certain level of fear of abandonment and rejection. Where possible, it is important to avoid direct criticism, opting instead to apply more encouraging expressions when addressing them and referring indirectly to the areas where you feel they ought to have done more and required further improvement.

Their colleagues should also try and ensure they do not allow themselves to talk down on other workers when around them or discuss situations that they may interpret as being indirectly targeted at them. When dealing with persons with BPD, it is always better to do more of listening than talking, by actually paying attention and ensuring that the issues they raise, especially when valid are acted on as soon as possible.

This can have the ripple effect of making them feel appreciated and important which can motivate them to put in that extra effort towards making the job or task a success.

If you have read my book on "Lonely Road", a book that tries to get into the head of how the thoughts inside the head of a person with BPD, you will find that a BPD person is also a victim of the circumstances in which he finds his or herself.

It is for this reason and more importantly to ensure the workplace continues to be productive that these steps aimed at helping people with borderline personality disorders at work must be respected by both employers and employees at the workplace.

A person with BPD can become defensive and begin to act irrationally if he or she feels singled out for improper behavior at work, so everything must be done to help them achieve productivity and aid them in their healing process.

Coworkers should understand that it is very important to keep their behavior professional at the workplace and be good examples to BPD persons. Talks around them should always be about the expectation on the job rather than on individual preferences. It is also important not to focus on the BPD aspect of their identity when addressing issues that concern their behavior.

Chapter Six

Certain Rights Enjoyed by an Employee with Borderline Personality Disorder

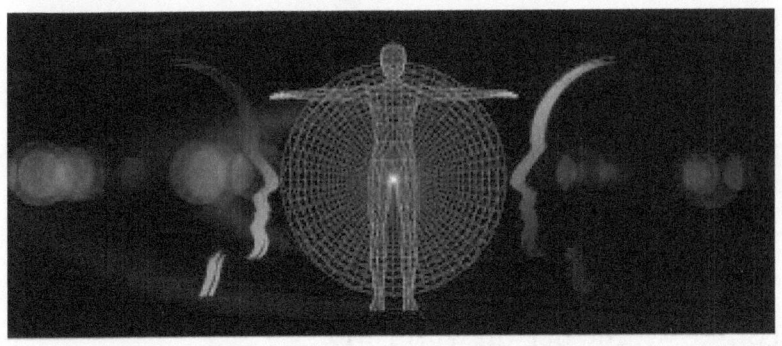

When it comes to the issue of legal rights and obligations, every country and even states have their own laws, so it is important to always verify before taking any actions with regard to what your rights entail.

Many states and nations have some form of legal protection for people who have mental or personality disorders. This helps ensure their rights are not trampled upon, and that they can fulfill what is expected of them for them to enjoy their own right.

Some countries and states have laws that protect a person with mental illness against discrimination for all aspects of their employment, recruitment, working hours, and even instances of termination or redundancy.

In many cases, it may not be necessary for an employee with a borderline personality disorder to disclose their mental health condition to a current or prospective employer, especially when it does not have a direct impact on the kind of job they are being employed to do. Even in cases when such disclosures are made, the employer may be obligated to respect and ensure it is kept private in most cases. The information can only be revealed or distributed with the consent of the person with BPD.

The disability rights laws or acts in many states posits that employers can treat mental illness as they would deal with physical illness, by ensuring a similar level of adjustments is made for them, so that the employees can continue to work while managing their conditions in the process. The objective of this is to ensure fairness and equity to avoid victimization in the workplace.

Employers also have the obligation of providing safe and healthy workplaces, conducive working conditions, and a system in place to encourage a safe working place where workers with mental health issues can disclose their conditions, especially when it impacts on their ability to work effectively. It would also sometimes be necessary for a superior officer or employers to run a risk assessment on employees with BPD to determine the adjustments to be made to ensure their productivity and safety at work.

To maintain a healthy workplace and also ensure that the rights of an employee with BPD are not trampled on, employers should endeavor to eliminate or minimize some common triggers to mental health issues, such as harassment, bullying, stress, workplace trauma or any form of assault by co-workers.

The essential way of handling mental illness in the workplace majorly boils down to the answer to two very important concepts;

- Can the employee (in this case, a BPD) meet the 'inherent requirements' of the job?
- Can the employer make 'necessary adjustments' to those requirements that would ensure that the employee works?

These adjustments, in this case, are expected to be reasonable and not designed to cause unjustifiable hardship for the employer.

Sometimes, these necessary adjustments can be simple and not too difficult to achieve. It can include;

- Sometimes working from home
- Designing a flexible work schedule
- Permission to speak with a health officer on the phone during work hours

Persons with BPD issues are also expected to assume a lot of responsibilities for their actions and not see it as an excuse to affect the workplace negatively. They are also expected to put in the efforts to make the adjustment made in their workplace to be effective. They should not forget that an employer has the right to terminate the appointment of anyone, including that of the BPD's appointment, if the terms of their work description are not met and they do not measure up to a level of performance expected of them.

Employees, including BPD employees, have a right to sue if they feel justifiably aggrieved about their work.

Chapter Seven

Steps on Being Productive as a BPD at the Workplace

It is possible for a person diagnosed with borderline personality disorder to be an effective employee and be productive.

Even though the social aspects of a person with borderline personality disorder may seem to negatively impact on them, they are however able to stay and work for long periods on a job without the drama of quitting suddenly.

Many persons with BPD are known to be very creative, intelligent and talented, sometimes in their own sort of way. They can beat the odds and go on to lead successful careers, even managing large team of experts and projects. The condition does not translate to not be fit for a job as a prospective employee. As with other similar conditions, it involves managing the illness so that the capabilities of the individual can better shine through. BPD is a lot more rampant than most people may realize. It is believed to be even more commonplace than bipolar disorder and schizophrenia combined. Chances are, you know someone with borderline personality disorder and may even have worked with someone who has BPD without realizing that they have BPD.

For a BPD person to lead an effective and productive lifestyle at work, they must consider the kind of job they are going for and the kind of work environment they will be in when working. There is a tendency for everyone to have something they are more passionate about over other things, things they really enjoy doing and even when challenges come up along the way. In spite of such challenging moments, persons who enjoy what they do tend not to mind, because they enjoy what they do.

Where possible, a person with BPD should make an effort to work in places or take up job offers that offer them opportunities in the fields where they have a lot of passion for.

For example, for someone that loves being around animals, they may feel a lot more productive working in places where they can be involved in the care of animals like as a veterinary or animal minder. Ditto for other applicable situations. The tendency to feel depressed and see a need to quit from a job you really enjoy will be low, since that is one challenge that many persons with BPD face.

A lot of people show up to work every day despite battling mental illness and still manage to make productive employees of themselves and run successful businesses. Do not just go for any job just for the sake of earning a living, instead aim to solve problems assigned to you.

Once you are diagnosed or suspect you have BPD, it is important to know that you will need to make a lot of reasonable adjustments at work, so letting your superiors know about your mental health condition may benefit you on the long run as they will have an idea of what to expect from you and become better equipped at dealing with you.

The responsibility of managing a mental health condition remains the responsibility of the person with the condition and not that of the employer. The employer may be required to be more understanding or be sympathetic to the condition of anyone who suffers from the symptoms of BPD and do whatever they can to help their workers manage their mental health issues since it would be everyone's benefit if the welfare of employees is placed on top priority.

People with BPD tend to be all too often associated with high-conflict, negativism, or divisive nature, because of this, many employers who understand what being with the BPD entails tend to put conditions in place to ensure you do not begin to affect other employees negatively, it is therefore important that you make a conscious effort to obey all the rules that have been stated and agreed with you so as to reduce any workplace drama.

As a person with BPD, talking to someone when there is a trigger is an important part of your healing process, however, knowing who you talk to is equally an important aspect of your being able to manage your disorder at work.

You should also learn to resist the temptation of mixing your domestic life with your official life. However, it is important to be friendly with your colleagues and try to derive fun while at work, so that the pressure of working can seem less like work.

You also have to learn what aspects of your life that should be kept private so that you do not feel vulnerable from opening too much to fellow employees. Sharing your previous suicide attempt or other personal business with fellow staff can make your private matter becomes a topic of discussion among members of staff whom you work with. Very often, even if you have previously trusted the person, you may suddenly start feeling that you are the object of any discussion around the office once you see them gather together, even if those discussions have nothing to do with you. Your condition will cause you to frequently idealize or demonize the persons you deal with including your colleagues, so that those you had previously trusted, you may eventually find that you are no longer comfortable with some of them. Even if you do not yet have a reason ever distrust anyone, the nature of BPD may lead you to eventually regret some of your past friendships. It is important to recognize this aspect of yourself in advance, before they actually occur. You are likely to be better off finding someone outside of the work environment with whom you can discuss your private affairs. However, no rule says you cannot find a good friend among any of your colleagues, as a matter of fact, a lot of people have grown to have a strong buddy from people whom they work with. You only have to be careful when involved in such situations.

Whether you are having an intense like or even love for a co-worker or a sudden hatred or dislike, you can take that feeling to this outside source, such as a therapist or a reliable friend, rather than to the person you work with. Do not forget that extreme feelings about others tend to be common with persons with BPD and tend to be fleeting. You also have to watch the potential of you causing division among other workers rather than them causing conflicts for you.

Set realistic goals for yourself at work, and include in those goals the development of stable, good and professional relationships. You can observe what others are doing and learn what these kinds of relationships take and put into consideration that this is an important aspect of your job.

Many people may feel distressed over not being as far along on their personal achievement ladder as they want to be, and in many ways this disappointment can affect their happiness and relationship with others. As a BPD, having the right relationships important to ensuring a healthy work environment may be difficult for you, but by working hard and being extremely committed to learning to recognize your own emotional reactivity along, with effective ways of coping can help you learn to react to others better.

One thing about BPD to be aware of, is that, you can get better, especially as you begin to age. You should always try and take advantage of every opportunity to learn from your past experiences and use it as a springboard to become a better person when tackling stress in other to avoid impulsive reactions.

Another way a BPD can handle stress at work is to resist the urge of quitting or having impulsive or intense reactions. You can manage your stress level by breaking down projects that are demanding into smaller chunks or bits. This way, the task at hand will feel smaller and make it seem as if you have less work to do instead of having the feeling of being punished with a huge task.

BPD persons are often faced with emotional deregulation that makes them have erratic mood swings, suicidal gestures, self-harm and sensitivity to problems in relationships. This experience can be overwhelming, resulting in difficulty managing those responses by BPD as a result of the very strong emotional stimulus. This tends to result in trying to handle it in ways that are mostly unhealthy to cope with the emotional pains such as the use of substance, alcohol, indiscriminate sex and even violence. This is very wrong as it may end up hurting you instead of offering relief. So as a BPD person, never resort to the use of substances (drugs or stimulants) or alcohol as a way of escaping from the reactions that come with the disorder. Instead, you should employ the different coping skills discussed earlier to be more productive and stable at work and in other spheres of life.

Keeping a logbook or journal, of what your aggressions or triggers are can help you keep tabs on your feelings. In doing this, you can devise better ways of handling similar situations when next you find yourself in such a condition again. Let us say you are faced with the struggle of identity, having that feeling of being worthless, hated or not being liked, you can write down what you feel and what made you feel that way. Then you can find possible ways to handle the feeling when it comes up again. Some people would take pictures of themselves and admire it when they start having that feeling of lack of identity. If this works for you, you can record it in the journal. So, when you are at work and someone's corrections tend to make you doubt yourself, all you have to do is check your diary and take note of the solution, which is to take pictures of yourself and admire it, until the feeling passes.

Issues or even arguments must come up in gatherings of people, especially at work, so, when someone's actions trigger or upsets you at work, instead of doing something impulsive or blowing up, simply remove yourself from the situation and wait for some seconds before reacting or responding. Remember that BPD can feed you with the wrong impression and that this feeling is fleeting. This way you end up thinking before you act. In the end, you might realize the issue is not worth being worked up about. You end up not causing any chaos at work or having an unnecessary conflict with a colleague. Doing this regularly reduces the possibility of you wanting to leave the job, thereby increasing the chances of getting along with your coworkers and staying long at the job.

One coping skill that can really help a borderline personality disorder person be very productive at work is being engaged. When faced with enraged feelings, instead of acting on them or releasing the outburst, you should try and get yourself busy. You can start up that task you are lagging behind on or that new task you have just been given. Better still, you can arrange the office, put the scattered files in their place, do the abandoned recordings, arrange the racks, or so many other chores in the office rather than stay passive. Doing this helps you stay active in your job and ensures you are productive.

As a BPD person, you should know that missing your treatment suggestion is not an option at any point. Be it psychotherapy or even medical treatments as directed by your doctor or therapist. Be consistent with your treatment so that your mental condition can be put in check and also helps you manage the defects that are associated with it. If you start missing your treatment, you run the risk of having emotional deregulation that can ruin your work life. No one would want to retain an employee that is always causing conflict in the workplace. The essence of your treatments will always be to help you develop ways of handling your emotions, developing how to better relate and get along with your coworkers. All these helps you to bring out the best of yourself and also help you sustain your job.

Creative Ways of Handling Some BPD Symptoms

These are some feelings BPDs battle with and possible ways you can tackle or go through them positively;

When Angry, Frustrated or Restless

Rip up an old newspaper, put on a headset and listen to soothing music, but if in the house, hit a pillow on the bed, smash ice cubes, engage in some rigorous exercises, do a physical activity like gardening, woodworks, house chores or even try out boxing a heavy bag.

When Depressed, Sad or Lonely

Write out all your negative thoughts on a sheet of paper and then tear it up when through. Then try and listen to a song that you find soothing. You can also write a comforting letter to the part of you that feels sad or alone. If it happens when you are at home, you can wrap yourself up in a blanket and watch your favorite TV show, play with a toy or cuddle your dog or cat.

When Anxious, in Panic, or Tensed

You can make a hot drink for yourself and take it slowly. You can inhale a smell, savor the taste, admire the shape of the mug and feel its weight in your hand. You can also take in ten deep breaths and start counting each of them aloud. You can take advantage of the logbook we discussed earlier and write down the things you can think of that describes your present situation, including such details as the time, date, color of the walls and type of furniture in the room. And if the feelings occur when you are at home, you can take a warm bath or shower, so that your mood is better regulated and help you change how your mood is by creating a soothing atmospheric condition and physical sensation to distract you from the negative feelings building up.

Having Dissociative Feeling or Spaced Out

You can chew a piece of ginger or chili, snap your feed on the ground, or drink a glass of ice-cold water.

Having Self-Harm Tendencies

Rub ice on the exact spot where you have the urge to hurt yourself. You can also stick an adhesive tape or a plaster on your skin and then peel it after a while. If that doesn't help, you can wear a rubber band or hairband on your wrist and snap it to feel some pain in a way that can shift your focus back to reality. If you are at home instead, you can take a cold bath.

These are a few of the ways of managing and handling your emotions and are real-life solutions that are known to have worked for people going through BPD. You can explore other healthy ways that work for you and write them down in your logbook. The major thing is having the mindset that borderline personality disorder is not a sentence to being useless or hopeless. You can still achieve your dreams and reach great heights in life, even with being diagnosed with this mental condition.

You can have great relationships with people, do well at a job and be productive if you would only put your mind to it. You can learn to manage your feelings following the steps mentioned in this study. With the above-mentioned practical guidelines, a BPD can stay long in a job and also become one of the most effective employees in the workplace.

Conclusion

Borderline Personality Disorder is a kind of personality disorder that pushes an individual to impulsive and intense unstable emotions. This makes it difficult for people who have it to maintain good relationships with people they work with. This begins to affect their work-life as the possibility of them maintaining or staying long in a job becomes low.

The cause of this personality disorder is traced to distressing childhood experiences and genetics. The major treatment required for possible recovery is psychotherapy and sometimes medications in managing the symptoms.

The job of a person with BPD is at constant risk of termination as the feelings that invariably come with this mental condition can typically make them cause chaos in the workplace. Some coping skills are suggested which could assist them to push through, enjoy a healthy relationship with coworkers, stay long in the job and also be productive at work. Some of those skills include; playing music, helping others, grounding yourself, engaging in activities, prayers, finding support, and writing down their feelings. The employer and colleagues of an individual with BPD also have a lot to do, because no matter how much effort, the individual puts into managing their mental condition, if they do not help out, not much success will be achieved.

Finally, borderline personality disorder is not the end of the road for anybody. A lot of them are in the workforce and are managing their condition very well. With the proper treatment, you can be a force to reckon with at your job. BPD does not restrain you from being productive or being your best at work.

www.ingramcontent.com/pod-product-compliance
Lightning Source LLC
Chambersburg PA
CBHW030526220526
45463CB00007B/2742